Creating and working with Charm Oracles

Fiona Beth Phillips

2021

Copyright 2021
Fiona Beth Phillips

All rights reserved. No part of this book may be reproduced in any form or by any electronic or mechanical means, including information storage and retrieval systems, without permission in writing from the publisher, except by reviewers, who may quote brief passages in a review.

Welcome Seer

In this book we are going to explore the magic and wisdom of charm oracles.

Oracles have been used for thousands of years to help us steer our path through life and connect to the mystery that is around and beyond us.

You will learn about creating your own charm oracle, divining meanings for your charms, carrying out charm oracle readings and using your charms with other oracles such as tarot and oracle cards.

In addition I provide possible meanings for some charms to get you started on your charming quest.

Your Toolkit

To begin we need to gather a few resources.

Your essentials are your charms.

You may already have these through crafting or you can start with a mixed bag which are readily available and reasonably priced from online suppliers. Alternatively you might have a Charmed Oracle set purchased from a creator and are looking to divine your own meanings.

In addition you may find it helpful to have:

A bag, pouch or tin to keep your charms in.

A notebook and pen to record your divinations.

Incense, oil or water to bless your charms.

A small tumbled stone such as clear quartz, amethyst or fluorite to keep alongside your charms to help them stay energetically shiny.

Getting Ready

"Divination is a means of telling ourselves
what we already know."
Joanne Harris

Gather your tools together.

Sort through your charms and pick out those which grab your
attention, the ones you are drawn to. Put the remainder and
duplicates to one side.
Set up your sacred space.
You might like to set out a small cloth to work on, light a candle, burn
some incense or have some crystal allies with you to help you as you
work.
Take three deep breaths.
Allow your body to relax and soften. If you wish to take a few
minutes to meditate or listen to some calming music.
When you are ready call in your guides and angels, deities you work
with or ancestors.
Ask them for guidance and insight as you work.

Divining Your Charm Meanings

Now take one charm at a time and study it.
Ask yourself these questions:

What does this object bring to mind?
What words jump out when I look at it?
Are there any phrases or songs which comes to mind? For instance, if
I pull a charm which is a high-heeled shoe I hear "walk tall".
What stories do I know about this charm - for example if you pull an
anchor or a fairy?
How does it make me feel?

This is your oracle, so work with what arises for you.
You may want to split this work over several days, channelling
messages can be heady work.

When you finish your session make sure to ground yourself with
something to eat and drink or a walk around your home barefoot.

Dedicating Your Charms

Once you have divined the meanings for your charms you might want to dedicate and bless them.

Create a simple ritual in which you bless your charms for use in oracle reading.

Pass them through smoke to cleanse them or send Reiki or white light to them to prepare them for use. Sit them out in the full moon or surround them with your favourite crystals...

Use the words here, or make up your own prayer as you are guided.

Divine Grace
Bless these charms
May they be a tool to aid
Clear knowing
Clear speaking
Clear listening
Clear understanding
May they support me in my oracle readings
Giving guidance, insight and wisdom
Under the law of grace
For the highest good of all.

So may it be.

Reading with Charms

Charms can be used on their own or with other oracle tools such as tarot. As with any form of divination give yourself time for quiet before you begin and call on your divine helpers for guidance.

One Charm Reading

Pull one charm at random for a simple message. Alternatively allow your eye to be drawn to whichever charm "jumps out" at you for daily guidance.

Three Charm Reading

Pick three charms and set them out in a row.

What message do they give together?

For instance, I pick an anchor, a bird and a rose...

Based on my divined meanings for my charms I could read this message as "Get grounded before you fly off in a different direction, if you do this there will be growth and beauty."

Casting Charms

Another way to read charms is to cast them.

To cast you need a casting mat or cloth.

Below is an example of a casting mat to explore wellbeing.

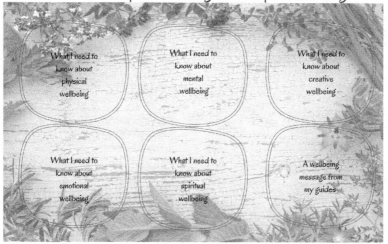

Prepare for your reading.

Next take a small pinch of charms (too many and you will find it hard to read the message as there will be so much information!)

Notice where the charms fall. For instance the sword falls on the emotional wellbeing square so I know I need to look at cutting cords. The leaf falls on the physical wellbeing square which tells me to pay attention to how I am nourishing myself.

If a charm falls between squares it indicates that it pertains to both areas. If a square is left blank then that is an area which currently does not need attention.

Using Charms with Other Oracles

Charms make a great companion in readings with other oracles, such as tarot.

When I read for clients I often pull charms alongside the cards to give additional depth to the message.

Let's have an example.

I pull the wheel of fortune. I want to know how my client should deal with the change they are facing.

When I pull a charm it is a crown, for me this means confidence. I can advise my client that although change is afoot they can be confident about how they approach this.

In another example I pull the fool. My client wants to know about their new beginning. I pull a key charm. This tells me that this fresh start will unlock something which has long been closed off for them.

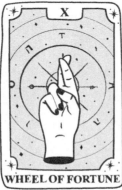

Next Steps

As with any new practice allow yourself to go slowly and enjoy the journey as you learn to work with your charms.

There is no "right" way to do this work. It depends on your own wisdom and experience, and those insights will allow you to create your own unique style of reading.

As time goes on you may wish to add to your charm set and expand the meanings you work with.

In the remainder of this book you will find suggested keywords for charms to get you started on your charmed oracle journey.

In time you may want to expand or change these as you come to know your own charms better.

A

Aeroplane - rise above this situation, travel, a long journey

Anchor - security, ride out the storm, something weighing you down, being stuck in place

Angel - divine guidance, blessings, seek connection to Spirit, be an angel for others

Arch - celebrate your achievements, victory, showing off

Arrow - focus, intention

Baby - inner child, pregnancy, parenthood, new beginnings

Bicycle - time to move on

Bird - spread your wings, if in a cage then freedom,

Boat - inner journeys, work with the unconscious

Butterfly - major transformation

C

Car - take charge of your direction

Castle - pull up the drawbridge

Cat - move with skill, take a nap, a familiar animal

Coin - money matters, finances, prosperity

Corn - harvest, seed for new planting

Crown - confidence, leadership

D

Devil - unhealthy patterns and choices, addictions

Dinosaur - history, old ideas, interesting but not useful

Dog - loyalty, animal allies

Dolphin - intuition, sacred play

E

Eiffel Tower - a new perspective,

Elephant - strength, remove obstacles, family

F

Fairy - connect to the earth elementals, seek enchantment, care for nature

Feather - cleanse and clear, messages in nature

Feet - grounding is needed, take the first step

Fish - go with the flow

Flower - a time of growth, bloom where you are planted

G
Goddess - connect to deity, grace

H
Hammer - get to work, using skills, building/ creating

Hand of Fatima - protection

Heart - healing, self care, love and relationships

Horse - personal power

Horseshoe - good fortune

House - domestic concerns, moving home, seeking a place of comfort

K
Key - unlocking, choosing to get yourself out of a blocked situation, seeking the means to help yourself

L
Leaf - be creative, release, nourish yourself

M
Mermaid - in-between, liminal, dream-work

Musical instruments - sing your own song

O
Owl - wisdom is needed, listen within, move carefully, hunt out what you need

P

Padlock - secrets, something is hidden, blocks

Pawprint - follow the signs

Peace Sign - call to activism

Pegasus - divine help is coming

S

Scissors - cut cords

Shell - gratitude, protection, natural gifts

Ship's Wheel - changes, cycles of life

Skull and crossbones - endings

Star - hope, destiny

Starfish - regeneration

T

Telephone - communication is needed, listen as well as speak

Turtle - go the distance, perseverance

W

Wild animals - work with the wild within

Witch's Hat - get your witch on

Y

Yin/ yang - karma, consequences, justice

For further study and exploration:

I first worked with charms during the Totally Spiritual course from New Age Hipster, you can find this class via the webstie:
https://www.newagehipster.co

For information on working with charms and magpie oracles you can explore Carrie Paris's work at:
https://carrieparis.com

Molly Remer also offers a class on Trinket Oracles via her website:
http://www.brigidsgrove.com/

I offer workshops on charm reading via my website, and also charm oracle kits and resources on Etsy: to find out more about my work follow the links at:
https://linktr.ee/fionabeth

Fiona Beth Phillips 2021

About the Author

Fiona has over twenty years experience in teaching and mentoring on spirituality.
She believes that each of us has a unique spark of divine magic within us, and our life's work is to unlock that magic.

She is a working witch and practical priestess and follows an earth-based spiritual path rooted in her Celtic ancestry and the folklore of the U.K.

She teaches about divination and traditional witchcraft and holds sacred, magical spaces via her Patreon.
You can find out more about Fiona via the links here:
https://linktr.ee/fionabeth

Printed in Great Britain
by Amazon